The Joy of
First Piano Collection

HAL•LEONARD®

Exclusive Distributors:
Hal Leonard
7777 West Bluemound Road, Milwaukee, WI 53213
Email: info@halleonard.com

Hal Leonard Europe Limited
42 Wigmore Street Marylebone, London, WIU 2 RY
Email: info@halleonardeurope.com

Hal Leonard Australia Pty. Ltd.
4 Lentara Court Cheltenham, Victoria 9132, Australia
Email: info@halleonard.com.au

Order No. AM952765
ISBN 0-7119-7292-3
This book © Copyright 1998 by Hal Leonard

Music compiled and arranged by Stephen Duro.
Music processed by Allegro Reproductions.
Cover illustration by Ian Beck.

Printed in the EU

www.halleonard.com

Hot Cross Buns

Traditional

Jolly

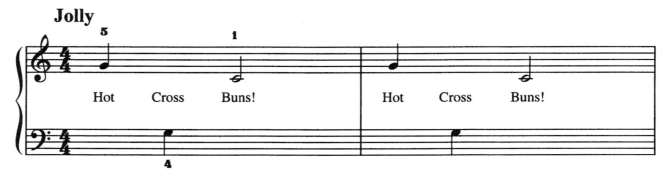

Hot Cross Buns! Hot Cross Buns!

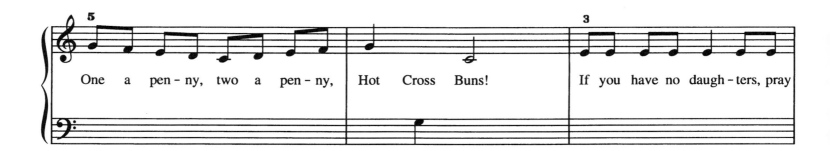

One a pen - ny, two a pen - ny, Hot Cross Buns! If you have no daugh - ters, pray

give them to your sons, One a pen - ny, two a pen - ny, Hot Cross Buns!

Baa! Baa! Black Sheep

Traditional

Moderately

Baa, Baa, black sheep, have you a - ny wool? Yes, sir, yes, sir,

three bags full. One for my mas – ter, and one for my dame, and

one for the lit – tle boy who lives down the lane.

Hickory, Dickory Dock!
Traditional

Not too fast

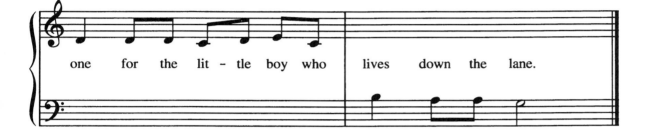

Hick – o – ry, Dick – o – ry Dock!___ The mouse___ ran up___ the clock.___ The

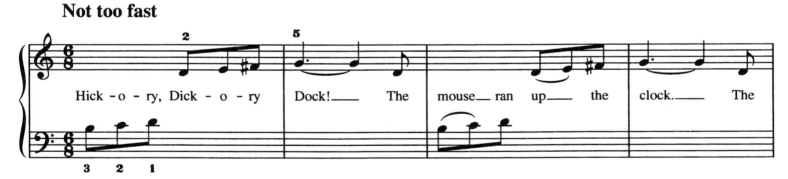

clock struck 'One', the mouse ran down, Hick – o – ry, Dick – o – ry Dock!

While Shepherds Watched Their Flocks By Night

Traditional

Moderately

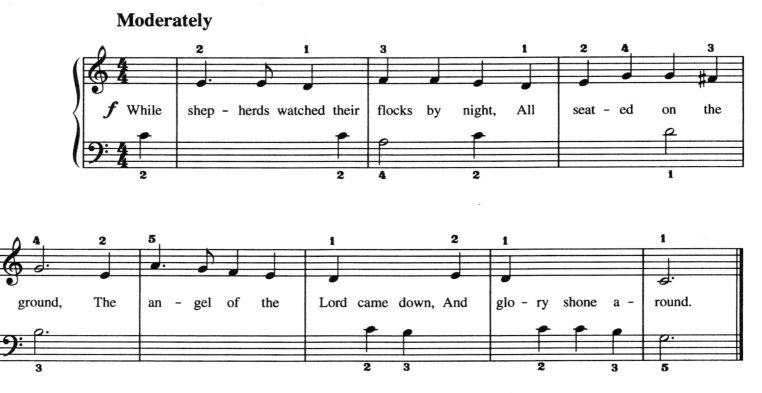

While shep - herds watched their flocks by night, All seat - ed on the ground, The an - gel of the Lord came down, And glo - ry shone a - round.

Jingle Bells

Traditional

Bright

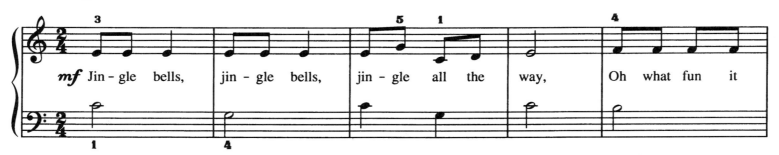

Jin - gle bells, jin - gle bells, jin - gle all the way, Oh what fun it

is to ride in a one horse o - pen sleigh.___ one horse op - en sleigh.

Old MacDonald Had A Farm

Traditional

Moderately

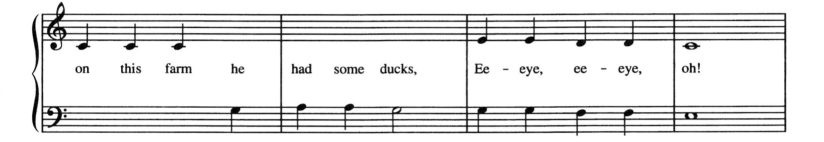

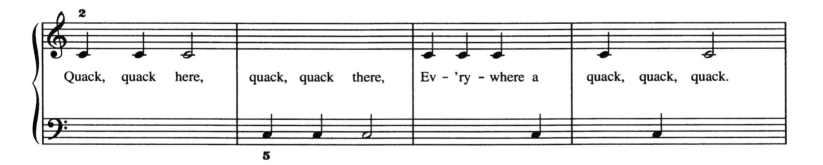

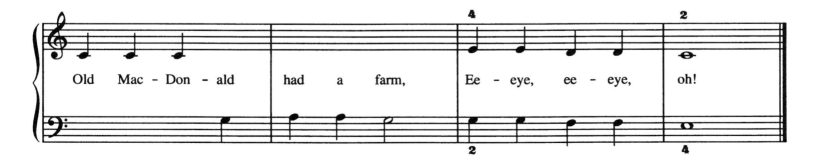

My Bonnie Lies Over The Ocean

Traditional

Moderately

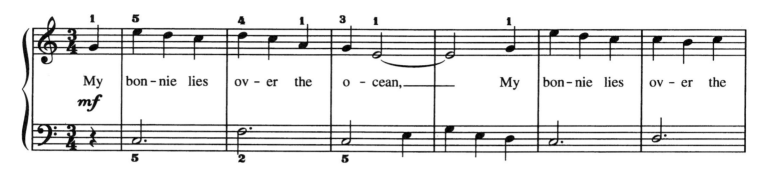

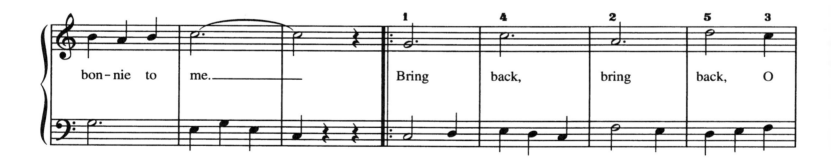

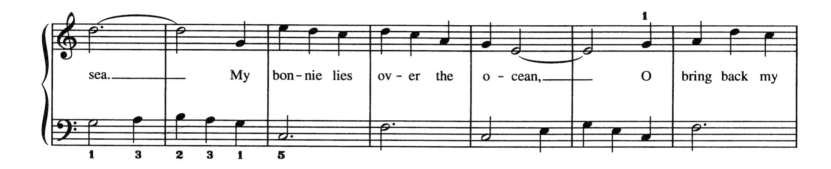

Little Bo-Peep

Traditional

Moderately

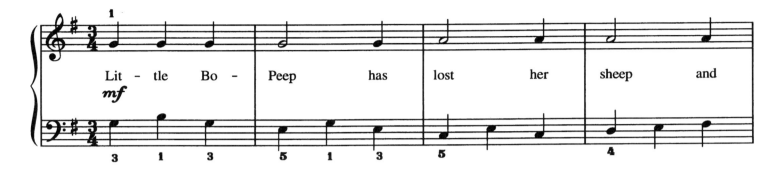

Lit - tle Bo - Peep has lost her sheep and

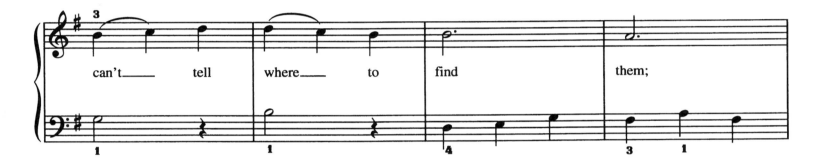

can't____ tell where____ to find them;

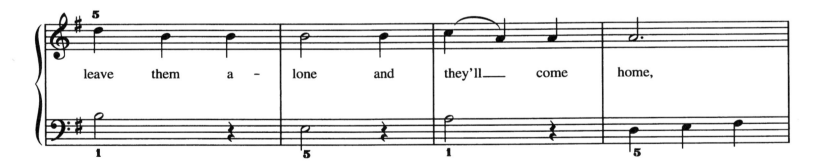

leave them a - lone and they'll____ come home,

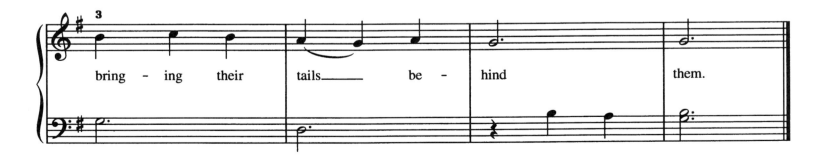

bring - ing their tails____ be - hind them.

Mary Had A Little Lamb

Traditional

Moderately bright

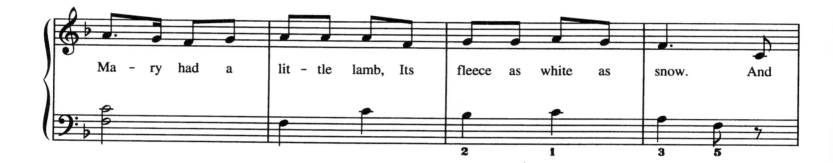

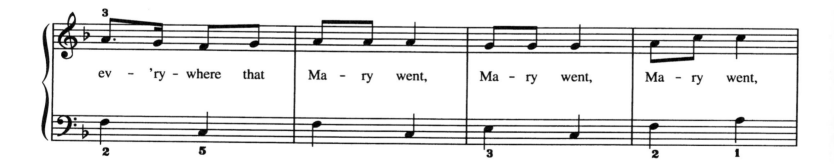

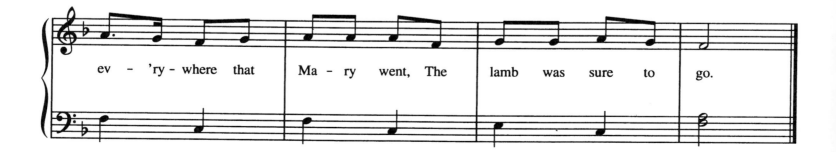

Polly Put The Kettle On

Traditional

Moderately bright

Pol - ly put the ket - tle on, Pol - ly put the ket - tle on,

mf

Pol - ly put the ket - tle on, We'll all have tea.

Su - key take it off a - gain, Su - key take it off a - gain,

Su - key take it off a - gain, They've all gone a - way.

Early One Morning

Traditional

Moderately

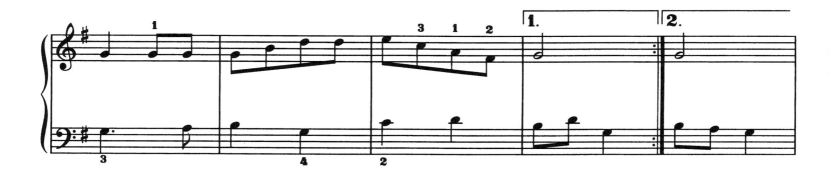

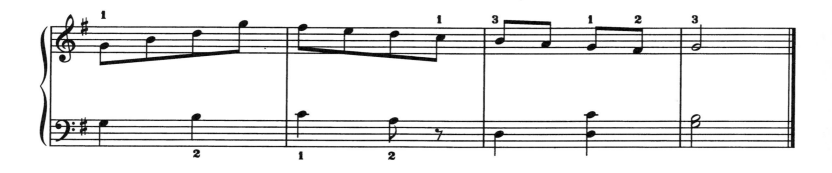

Gavotte

George Frideric Handel (1685-1759)

Andante

Old German Dance

Michael Praetorius (1571-1621)

Moderately

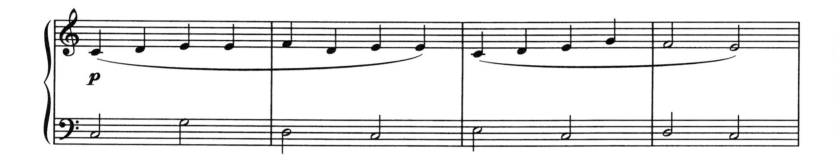

German Dance

Joseph Haydn (1732-1809)

Allegretto

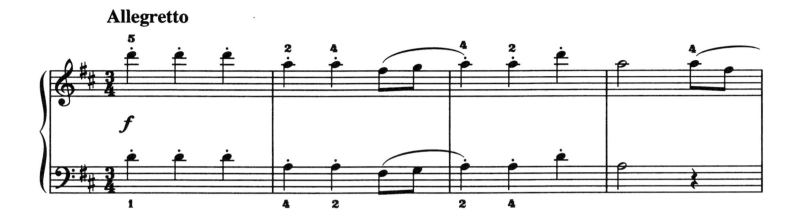

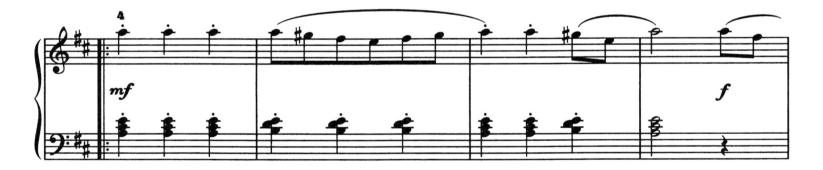

Minuet K.6

Wolfgang Amadeus Mozart (1756-1791)

Andante grazioso

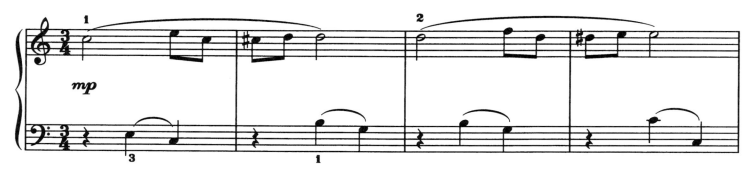

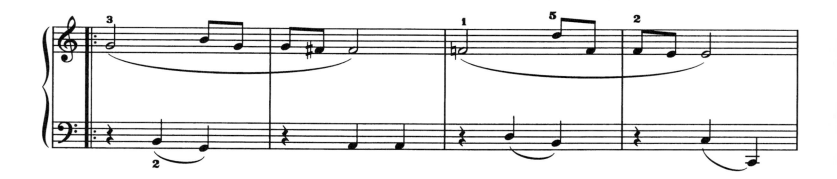

Air

Johann Gräfe (1711-1787)

Andante

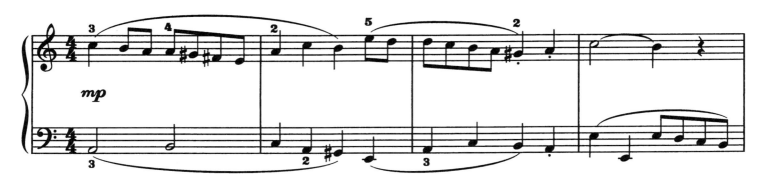

Minuet

Wilhelm Friedemann Bach (1710-1784)

Grazioso

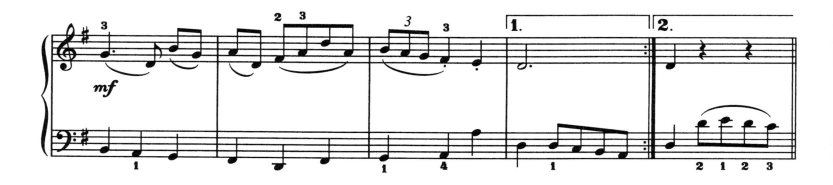

Andantino in F

Cornelius Gurlitt (1820-1901)

Andantino

Old German Lullaby

Johann Phillip Kirnberger (1721-1283)

Moderately

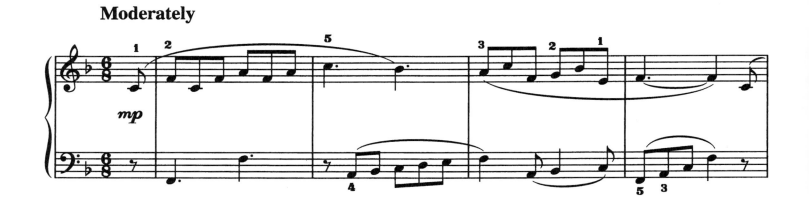

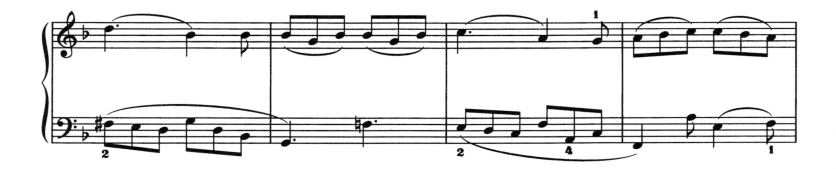

Elegy

Carl Reinecke (1824-1910)

Andante con moto

The Ash Grove

Traditional

Moderately

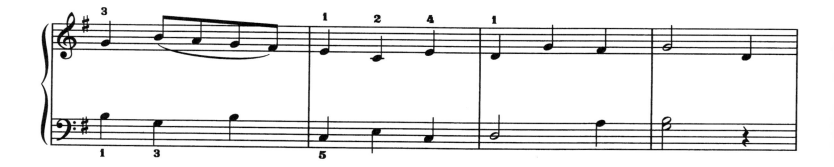

Minuet

Johann Sebastian Bach (1685-1750)

Andante con moto

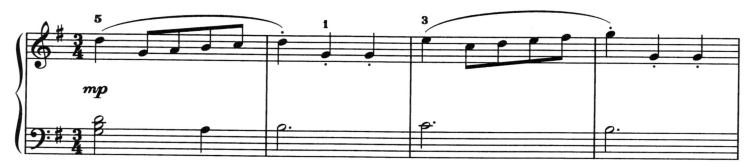

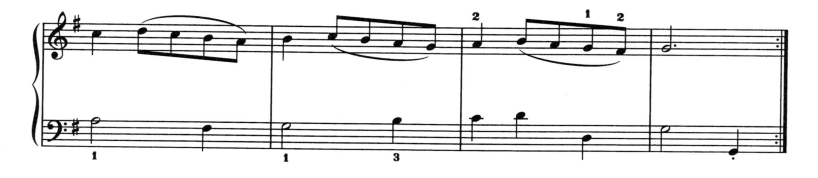

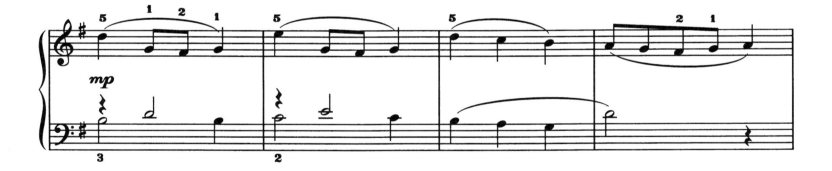

Greensleeves

Traditional

Flowing

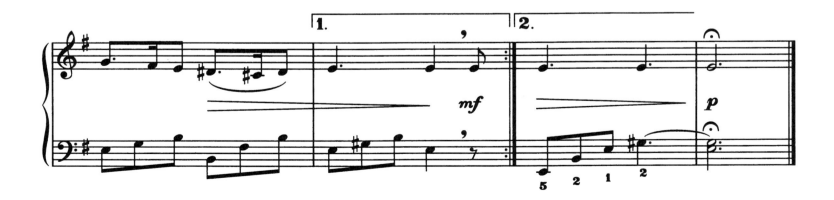

27

Playful Dialogue

Johann Nepomuk Hummel (1778-1837)

Moderately

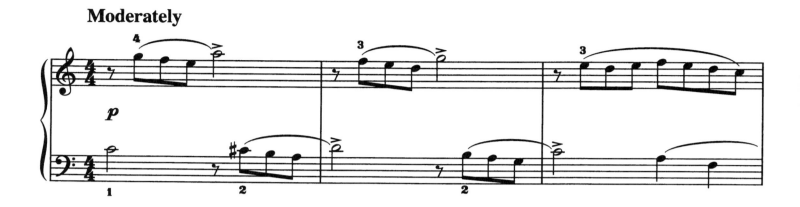

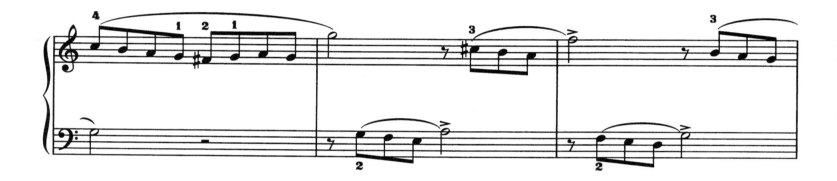

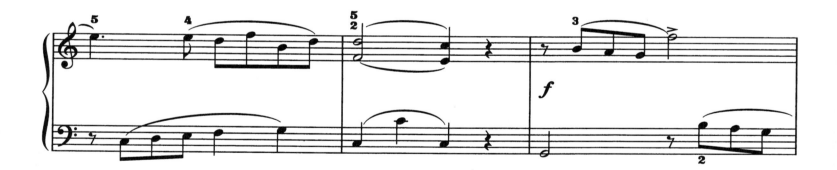

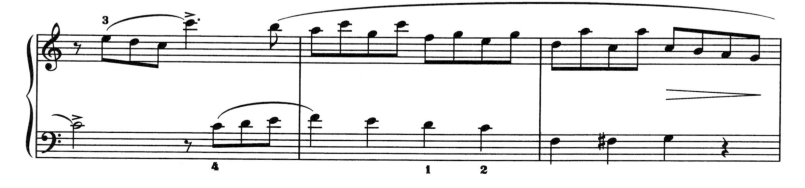

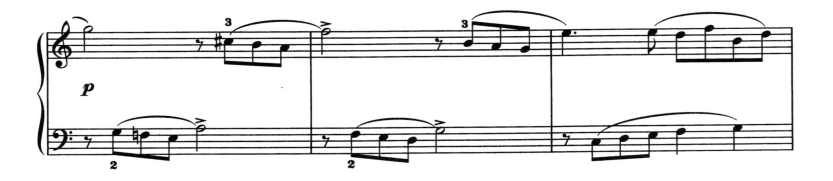

Burlesca

Wolfgang Amadeus Mozart (1756-1791)

Allegretto

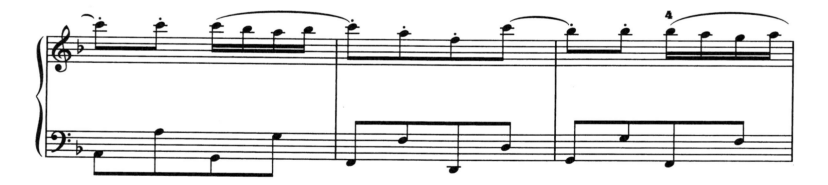

Romanza

Daniel Steibelt (1765-1823)

Andantino

Minuet in C

Richard Jones (d.1744)

Moderately

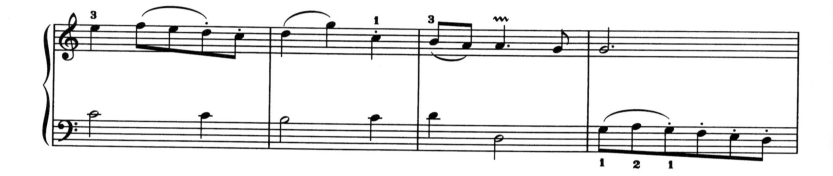

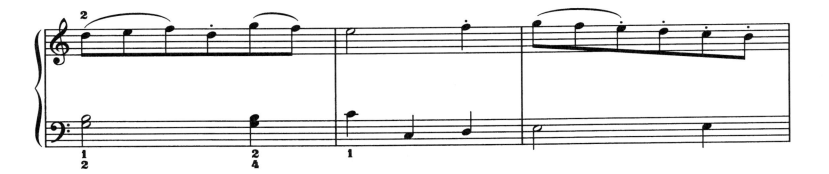

Sonatina in G

Ludwig van Beethoven (1770-1827)

Moderately

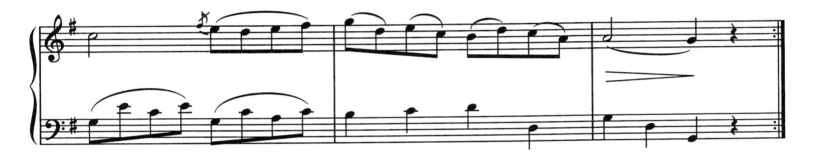

Menuet in D minor

Attributed to J.S. Bach (1685-1750)

Moderately

Games

Daniel Gottlob Türk (1756-1813)

Vivo

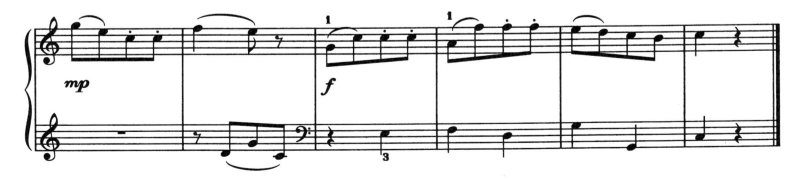

Rondo
From Sonatina No.1 in G

Thomas Attwood (1765-1858)

Allegro

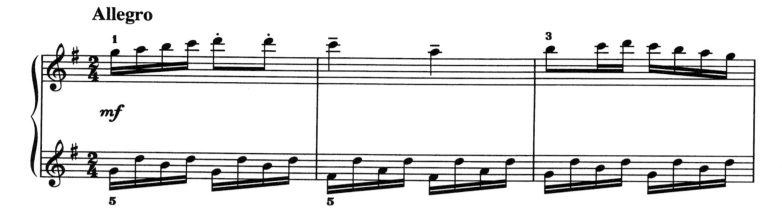

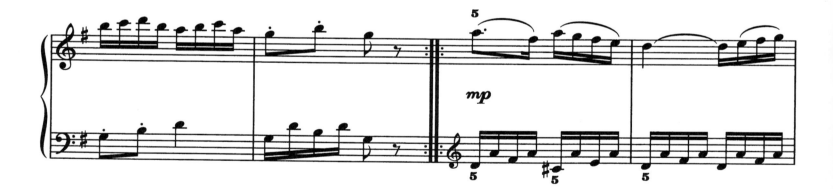

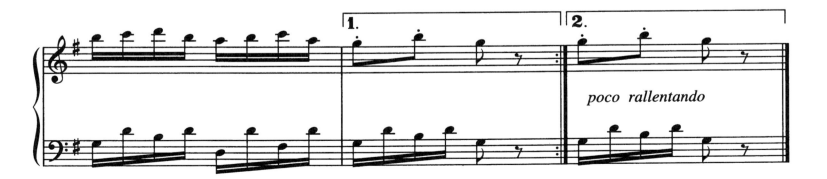

poco rallentando

Polonaise in G minor

Johann Sebastian Bach (1685-1750)

Moderately

Rondoletto

Christian Traugott Brunner (1792-1874)

Allegretto

Allegro
From Sonatina No.1 in G

Thomas Attwood (1765-1858)

Allegro

Scherzo in F

Johann Wilhelm Hässler (1747-1822)

Allegro

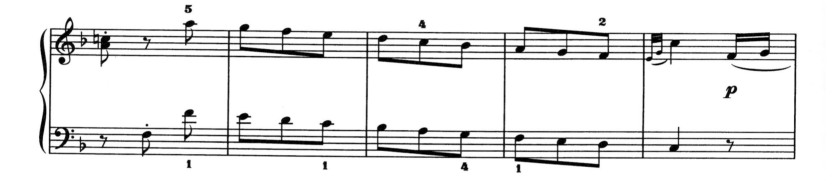

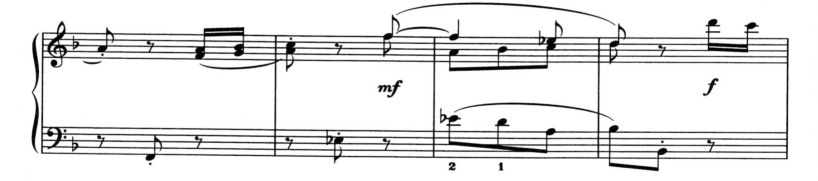

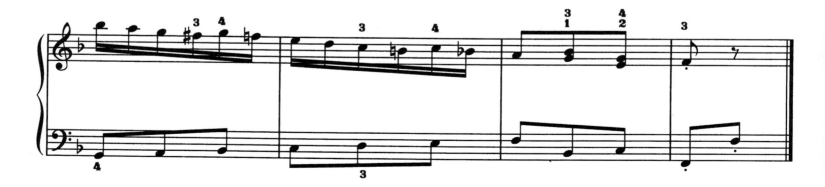

Canzone

Daniel Gottlob Türk (1756-1813)

Andantino

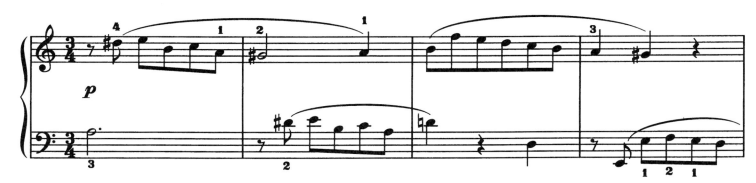

Musette

Johann Sebastian Bach (1685-1750)

Allegro moderato

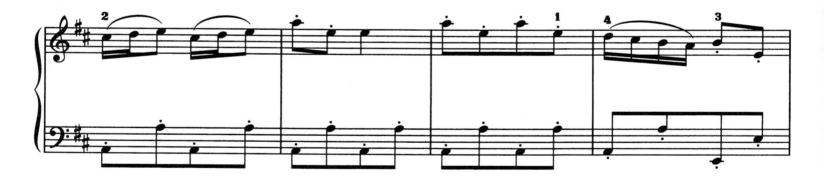

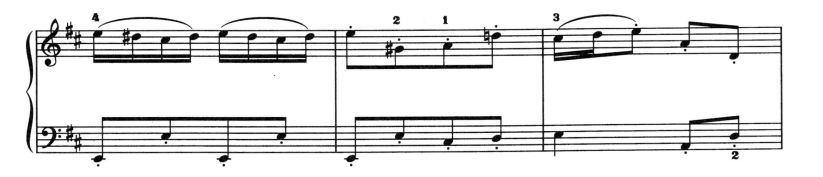

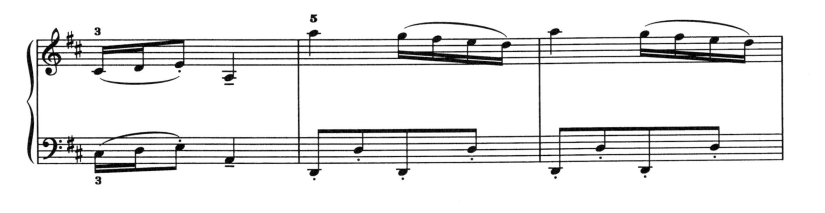

Menuet in G

Ludwig van Beethoven (1770-1827)

Fine

Trio

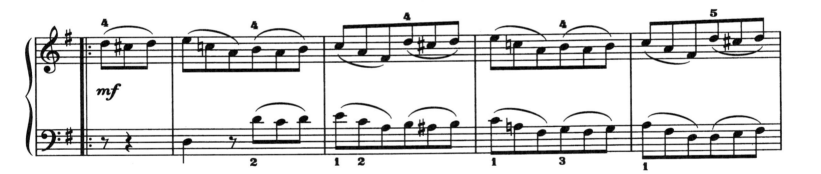

Menuet da Capo

Arabesque

Friedrich Burgmüller (1806-1874)

Allegro scherzando

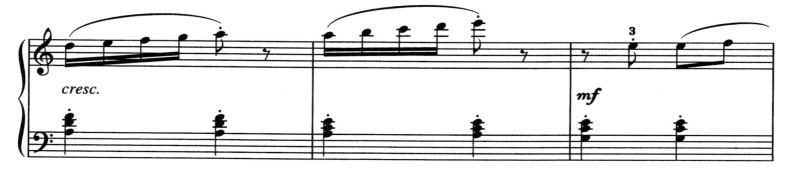

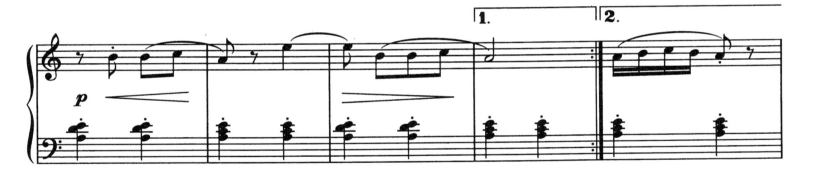

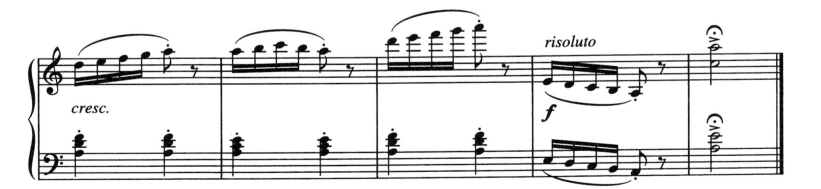

Menuet in C

Ludwig van Beethoven (1770-1827)

Moderately

Fine

Trio

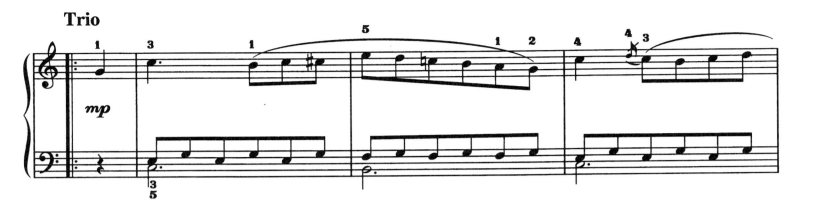

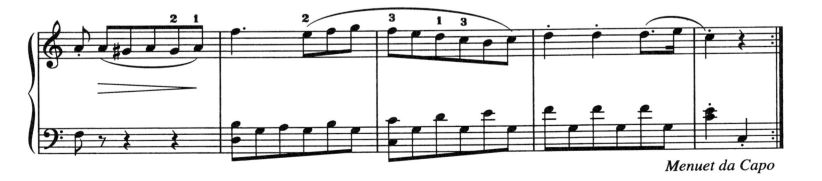

Menuet da Capo

57

Allegro
From Sonatina in F

Ludwig van Beethoven (1770-1827)

Allegro assai

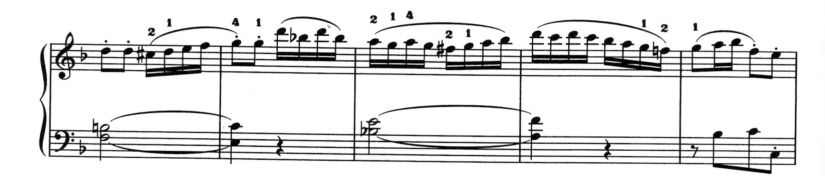

Prelude in C minor

Johann Sebastian Bach (1685-1750)

Andante

Waltz

Franz Schubert (1797-1828)

Moderately

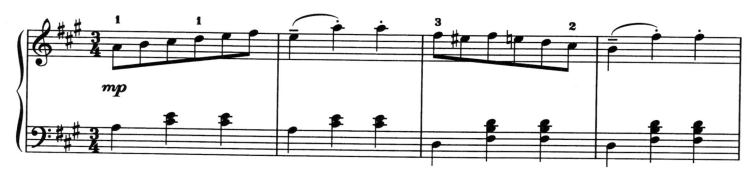